ADDRESS BOOK FOR PROFESSIONALS ON THE GO

Copyright 2013
978-1-63022-409-7
First Printed October 8, 2013

Speedy Publishing LLC
40 E. Main St., #1156, Newark, DE 19711

www.SpeedyPublishing.Co

NAME & ADDRESS

PHONE

_____

WORK
_____

FAX
_____

MOBILE
_____

HOME
_____

OTHER
_____

E-MAIL
_____

WORK
_____

FAX
_____

MOBILE
_____

HOME
_____

OTHER
_____

E-MAIL
_____

WORK
_____

FAX
_____

MOBILE
_____

HOME
_____

OTHER
_____

E-MAIL
_____

WORK
_____

FAX
_____

MOBILE
_____

HOME
_____

OTHER
_____

E-MAIL

NAME & ADDRESS

PHONE

WORK

FAX

MOBILE

HOME

OTHER

E-MAIL

WORK

FAX

MOBILE

HOME

OTHER

E-MAIL

WORK

FAX

MOBILE

HOME

OTHER

E-MAIL

WORK

FAX

MOBILE

HOME

OTHER

E-MAIL

NAME & ADDRESS

PHONE

WORK

FAX

MOBILE

HOME

OTHER

E-MAIL

WORK

FAX

MOBILE

HOME

OTHER

E-MAIL

WORK

FAX

MOBILE

HOME

OTHER

E-MAIL

WORK

FAX

MOBILE

HOME

OTHER

E-MAIL

NAME & ADDRESS

PHONE

WORK

FAX

MOBILE

HOME

OTHER

E-MAIL

WORK

FAX

MOBILE

HOME

OTHER

E-MAIL

WORK

FAX

MOBILE

HOME

OTHER

E-MAIL

WORK

FAX

MOBILE

HOME

OTHER

E-MAIL

NAME & ADDRESS

PHONE

WORK

FAX

MOBILE

HOME

OTHER

E-MAIL

WORK

FAX

MOBILE

HOME

OTHER

E-MAIL

WORK

FAX

MOBILE

HOME

OTHER

E-MAIL

WORK

FAX

MOBILE

HOME

OTHER

E-MAIL

NAME & ADDRESS

PHONE

WORK

FAX

MOBILE

HOME

OTHER

E-MAIL

WORK

FAX

MOBILE

HOME

OTHER

E-MAIL

WORK

FAX

MOBILE

HOME

OTHER

E-MAIL

WORK

FAX

MOBILE

HOME

OTHER

E-MAIL

NAME & ADDRESS

PHONE

WORK

_____

FAX

_____

MOBILE

_____

HOME

_____

OTHER

E-MAIL

_____

WORK

_____

FAX

_____

MOBILE

_____

HOME

_____

OTHER

E-MAIL

_____

WORK

_____

FAX

_____

MOBILE

_____

HOME

_____

OTHER

E-MAIL

_____

WORK

_____

FAX

_____

MOBILE

_____

HOME

_____

OTHER

E-MAIL

NAME & ADDRESS

PHONE

WORK

FAX

MOBILE

HOME

OTHER

E-MAIL

WORK

FAX

MOBILE

HOME

OTHER

E-MAIL

WORK

FAX

MOBILE

HOME

OTHER

E-MAIL

WORK

FAX

MOBILE

HOME

OTHER

E-MAIL

NAME & ADDRESS

PHONE

WORK

FAX

MOBILE

HOME

OTHER

E-MAIL

WORK

FAX

MOBILE

HOME

OTHER

E-MAIL

WORK

FAX

MOBILE

HOME

OTHER

E-MAIL

WORK

FAX

MOBILE

HOME

OTHER

E-MAIL

NAME & ADDRESS　　PHONE

WORK

FAX

MOBILE

HOME

OTHER

E-MAIL

WORK

FAX

MOBILE

HOME

OTHER

E-MAIL

WORK

FAX

MOBILE

HOME

OTHER

E-MAIL

WORK

FAX

MOBILE

HOME

OTHER

E-MAIL

NAME & ADDRESS

PHONE

WORK

FAX

MOBILE

HOME

OTHER

E-MAIL

WORK

FAX

MOBILE

HOME

OTHER

E-MAIL

WORK

FAX

MOBILE

HOME

OTHER

E-MAIL

WORK

FAX

MOBILE

HOME

OTHER

E-MAIL

NAME & ADDRESS

PHONE

WORK

FAX

MOBILE

HOME

OTHER

E-MAIL

WORK

FAX

MOBILE

HOME

OTHER

E-MAIL

WORK

FAX

MOBILE

HOME

OTHER

E-MAIL

WORK

FAX

MOBILE

HOME

OTHER

E-MAIL

NAME & ADDRESS

PHONE

WORK
_____

FAX
_____

MOBILE
_____

HOME
_____

OTHER
_____

E-MAIL

WORK
_____

FAX
_____

MOBILE
_____

HOME
_____

OTHER
_____

E-MAIL

WORK
_____

FAX
_____

MOBILE
_____

HOME
_____

OTHER
_____

E-MAIL

WORK
_____

FAX
_____

MOBILE
_____

HOME
_____

OTHER
_____

E-MAIL

NAME & ADDRESS

PHONE

WORK

FAX

MOBILE

HOME

OTHER

E-MAIL

WORK

FAX

MOBILE

HOME

OTHER

E-MAIL

WORK

FAX

MOBILE

HOME

OTHER

E-MAIL

WORK

FAX

MOBILE

HOME

OTHER

E-MAIL

NAME & ADDRESS PHONE

_____ WORK _____

_____ FAX _____

_____ MOBILE _____

_____ HOME _____

_____ OTHER _____

E-MAIL _____

_____ WORK _____

_____ FAX _____

_____ MOBILE _____

_____ HOME _____

_____ OTHER _____

E-MAIL _____

_____ WORK _____

_____ FAX _____

_____ MOBILE _____

_____ HOME _____

_____ OTHER _____

E-MAIL _____

_____ WORK _____

_____ FAX _____

_____ MOBILE _____

_____ HOME _____

_____ OTHER _____

E-MAIL _____

NAME & ADDRESS

PHONE

WORK

FAX

MOBILE

HOME

OTHER

E-MAIL

WORK

FAX

MOBILE

HOME

OTHER

E-MAIL

WORK

FAX

MOBILE

HOME

OTHER

E-MAIL

WORK

FAX

MOBILE

HOME

OTHER

E-MAIL

NAME & ADDRESS

PHONE

WORK

FAX

MOBILE

HOME

OTHER

E-MAIL

WORK

FAX

MOBILE

HOME

OTHER

E-MAIL

WORK

FAX

MOBILE

HOME

OTHER

E-MAIL

WORK

FAX

MOBILE

HOME

OTHER

E-MAIL

NAME & ADDRESS

PHONE

WORK

FAX

MOBILE

HOME

OTHER

E-MAIL

WORK

FAX

MOBILE

HOME

OTHER

E-MAIL

WORK

FAX

MOBILE

HOME

OTHER

E-MAIL

WORK

FAX

MOBILE

HOME

OTHER

E-MAIL

NAME & ADDRESS

PHONE

WORK

FAX

MOBILE

HOME

OTHER

E-MAIL

WORK

FAX

MOBILE

HOME

OTHER

E-MAIL

WORK

FAX

MOBILE

HOME

OTHER

E-MAIL

WORK

FAX

MOBILE

HOME

OTHER

E-MAIL

NAME & ADDRESS

PHONE

WORK

FAX

MOBILE

HOME

OTHER

E-MAIL

WORK

FAX

MOBILE

HOME

OTHER

E-MAIL

WORK

FAX

MOBILE

HOME

OTHER

E-MAIL

WORK

FAX

MOBILE

HOME

OTHER

E-MAIL

NAME & ADDRESS

PHONE

WORK

FAX

MOBILE

HOME

OTHER

E-MAIL

WORK

FAX

MOBILE

HOME

OTHER

E-MAIL

WORK

FAX

MOBILE

HOME

OTHER

E-MAIL

WORK

FAX

MOBILE

HOME

OTHER

E-MAIL

NAME & ADDRESS

PHONE

WORK

FAX

MOBILE

HOME

OTHER

E-MAIL

WORK

FAX

MOBILE

HOME

OTHER

E-MAIL

WORK

FAX

MOBILE

HOME

OTHER

E-MAIL

WORK

FAX

MOBILE

HOME

OTHER

E-MAIL

NAME & ADDRESS

PHONE

WORK

FAX

MOBILE

HOME

OTHER

E-MAIL

WORK

FAX

MOBILE

HOME

OTHER

E-MAIL

WORK

FAX

MOBILE

HOME

OTHER

E-MAIL

WORK

FAX

MOBILE

HOME

OTHER

E-MAIL

NAME & ADDRESS

PHONE

WORK

FAX

MOBILE

HOME

OTHER

E-MAIL

WORK

FAX

MOBILE

HOME

OTHER

E-MAIL

WORK

FAX

MOBILE

HOME

OTHER

E-MAIL

WORK

FAX

MOBILE

HOME

OTHER

E-MAIL

NAME & ADDRESS

PHONE

WORK _____

FAX _____

MOBILE _____

HOME _____

OTHER _____

E-MAIL _____

WORK _____

FAX _____

MOBILE _____

HOME _____

OTHER _____

E-MAIL _____

WORK _____

FAX _____

MOBILE _____

HOME _____

OTHER _____

E-MAIL _____

WORK _____

FAX _____

MOBILE _____

HOME _____

OTHER _____

E-MAIL _____

NAME & ADDRESS

PHONE

WORK

FAX

MOBILE

HOME

OTHER

E-MAIL

WORK

FAX

MOBILE

HOME

OTHER

E-MAIL

WORK

FAX

MOBILE

HOME

OTHER

E-MAIL

WORK

FAX

MOBILE

HOME

OTHER

E-MAIL

NAME & ADDRESS

PHONE

_____ WORK _____

_____ FAX _____

_____ MOBILE _____

_____ HOME _____

_____ OTHER _____

E-MAIL _____

_____ WORK _____

_____ FAX _____

_____ MOBILE _____

_____ HOME _____

_____ OTHER _____

E-MAIL _____

_____ WORK _____

_____ FAX _____

_____ MOBILE _____

_____ HOME _____

_____ OTHER _____

E-MAIL _____

_____ WORK _____

_____ FAX _____

_____ MOBILE _____

_____ HOME _____

_____ OTHER _____

E-MAIL _____

NAME & ADDRESS

PHONE

WORK

FAX

MOBILE

HOME

OTHER

E-MAIL

WORK

FAX

MOBILE

HOME

OTHER

E-MAIL

WORK

FAX

MOBILE

HOME

OTHER

E-MAIL

WORK

FAX

MOBILE

HOME

OTHER

E-MAIL

NAME & ADDRESS

PHONE

WORK

FAX

MOBILE

HOME

OTHER

E-MAIL

WORK

FAX

MOBILE

HOME

OTHER

E-MAIL

WORK

FAX

MOBILE

HOME

OTHER

E-MAIL

WORK

FAX

MOBILE

HOME

OTHER

E-MAIL

NAME & ADDRESS

PHONE

WORK

FAX

MOBILE

HOME

OTHER

E-MAIL

WORK

FAX

MOBILE

HOME

OTHER

E-MAIL

WORK

FAX

MOBILE

HOME

OTHER

E-MAIL

WORK

FAX

MOBILE

HOME

OTHER

E-MAIL

NAME & ADDRESS

PHONE

WORK

FAX

MOBILE

HOME

OTHER

E-MAIL

WORK

FAX

MOBILE

HOME

OTHER

E-MAIL

WORK

FAX

MOBILE

HOME

OTHER

E-MAIL

WORK

FAX

MOBILE

HOME

OTHER

E-MAIL

NAME & ADDRESS

PHONE

WORK

FAX

MOBILE

HOME

OTHER

E-MAIL

WORK

FAX

MOBILE

HOME

OTHER

E-MAIL

WORK

FAX

MOBILE

HOME

OTHER

E-MAIL

WORK

FAX

MOBILE

HOME

OTHER

E-MAIL

NAME & ADDRESS

PHONE

WORK

FAX

MOBILE

HOME

OTHER

E-MAIL

WORK

FAX

MOBILE

HOME

OTHER

E-MAIL

WORK

FAX

MOBILE

HOME

OTHER

E-MAIL

WORK

FAX

MOBILE

HOME

OTHER

E-MAIL

NAME & ADDRESS

PHONE

WORK

FAX

MOBILE

HOME

OTHER

E-MAIL

WORK

FAX

MOBILE

HOME

OTHER

E-MAIL

WORK

FAX

MOBILE

HOME

OTHER

E-MAIL

WORK

FAX

MOBILE

HOME

OTHER

E-MAIL

NAME & ADDRESS

PHONE

WORK

FAX

MOBILE

HOME

OTHER

E-MAIL

WORK

FAX

MOBILE

HOME

OTHER

E-MAIL

WORK

FAX

MOBILE

HOME

OTHER

E-MAIL

WORK

FAX

MOBILE

HOME

OTHER

E-MAIL

NAME & ADDRESS

PHONE

WORK

FAX

MOBILE

HOME

OTHER

E-MAIL

WORK

FAX

MOBILE

HOME

OTHER

E-MAIL

WORK

FAX

MOBILE

HOME

OTHER

E-MAIL

WORK

FAX

MOBILE

HOME

OTHER

E-MAIL

NAME & ADDRESS

PHONE

WORK

FAX

MOBILE

HOME

OTHER

E-MAIL

WORK

FAX

MOBILE

HOME

OTHER

E-MAIL

WORK

FAX

MOBILE

HOME

OTHER

E-MAIL

WORK

FAX

MOBILE

HOME

OTHER

E-MAIL

NAME & ADDRESS

PHONE

WORK

FAX

MOBILE

HOME

OTHER

E-MAIL

WORK

FAX

MOBILE

HOME

OTHER

E-MAIL

WORK

FAX

MOBILE

HOME

OTHER

E-MAIL

WORK

FAX

MOBILE

HOME

OTHER

E-MAIL

NAME & ADDRESS

PHONE

WORK

FAX

MOBILE

HOME

OTHER

E-MAIL

WORK

FAX

MOBILE

HOME

OTHER

E-MAIL

WORK

FAX

MOBILE

HOME

OTHER

E-MAIL

WORK

FAX

MOBILE

HOME

OTHER

E-MAIL

NAME & ADDRESS

PHONE

WORK

FAX

MOBILE

HOME

OTHER

E-MAIL

WORK

FAX

MOBILE

HOME

OTHER

E-MAIL

WORK

FAX

MOBILE

HOME

OTHER

E-MAIL

WORK

FAX

MOBILE

HOME

OTHER

E-MAIL

NAME & ADDRESS

PHONE

WORK

FAX

MOBILE

HOME

OTHER

E-MAIL

WORK

FAX

MOBILE

HOME

OTHER

E-MAIL

WORK

FAX

MOBILE

HOME

OTHER

E-MAIL

WORK

FAX

MOBILE

HOME

OTHER

E-MAIL

NAME & ADDRESS

PHONE

WORK

FAX

MOBILE

HOME

OTHER

E-MAIL

WORK

FAX

MOBILE

HOME

OTHER

E-MAIL

WORK

FAX

MOBILE

HOME

OTHER

E-MAIL

WORK

FAX

MOBILE

HOME

OTHER

E-MAIL

NAME & ADDRESS

PHONE

WORK

FAX

MOBILE

HOME

OTHER

E-MAIL

WORK

FAX

MOBILE

HOME

OTHER

E-MAIL

WORK

FAX

MOBILE

HOME

OTHER

E-MAIL

WORK

FAX

MOBILE

HOME

OTHER

E-MAIL

NAME & ADDRESS   PHONE

WORK

FAX

MOBILE

HOME

OTHER

E-MAIL

WORK

FAX

MOBILE

HOME

OTHER

E-MAIL

WORK

FAX

MOBILE

HOME

OTHER

E-MAIL

WORK

FAX

MOBILE

HOME

OTHER

E-MAIL

NAME & ADDRESS

PHONE

WORK

FAX

MOBILE

HOME

OTHER

E-MAIL

WORK

FAX

MOBILE

HOME

OTHER

E-MAIL

WORK

FAX

MOBILE

HOME

OTHER

E-MAIL

WORK

FAX

MOBILE

HOME

OTHER

E-MAIL

NAME & ADDRESS

PHONE

WORK

FAX

MOBILE

HOME

OTHER

E-MAIL

WORK

FAX

MOBILE

HOME

OTHER

E-MAIL

WORK

FAX

MOBILE

HOME

OTHER

E-MAIL

WORK

FAX

MOBILE

HOME

OTHER

E-MAIL

NAME & ADDRESS

PHONE

_____

_____

_____

_____

E-MAIL

WORK _____

FAX _____

MOBILE _____

HOME _____

OTHER _____

_____

_____

_____

_____

E-MAIL

WORK _____

FAX _____

MOBILE _____

HOME _____

OTHER _____

_____

_____

_____

_____

E-MAIL

WORK _____

FAX _____

MOBILE _____

HOME _____

OTHER _____

_____

_____

_____

_____

E-MAIL

WORK _____

FAX _____

MOBILE _____

HOME _____

OTHER _____

NAME & ADDRESS

PHONE

WORK

FAX

MOBILE

HOME

OTHER

E-MAIL

WORK

FAX

MOBILE

HOME

OTHER

E-MAIL

WORK

FAX

MOBILE

HOME

OTHER

E-MAIL

WORK

FAX

MOBILE

HOME

OTHER

E-MAIL